Arduino

A Beginner's Guide to Arduino Programming

Table of Contents

Introduction

We are living in an era of technological revolution where we encounter new inventions and innovations each day. The average number of people with technological literacy continues to rise as more and more people become versed in the hardware and software of this digital age.

Whether you are a dabbling hobbyist or a professional engineer, you may have heard of Arduino technology and have found an interest in it for one reason or another. Perhaps you have heard of the flexibility and ease of using it to build gadgets, or you may have seen a variety of projects built with Arduino technologies. And if that's not the case, then you may have seen some gadgets and wondered how they really worked. Remote control boats, vending machines, and the systems that control elevators or electronic toys all have foundations in Arduino.

Regardless of the reason, if you have an interest or a passion in knowing how Arduino technology operates and would love to use it at some point to design interesting projects for pleasure or for profit, you are in the right place. This book will help you do just that. But before we dive deeper, let's look at this Arduino thing and how it started.

What exactly is Arduino?

Arduino is a cheap, open-source electronics platform based on easy-to-use hardware and software used for building and controlling electronic objects and interactive systems. All Arduino boards use a microcontroller with additional electronic components to maintain the availability and durability of the computing unit. It also consists of an integrated development environment, IDE, where one can write and run the programs.

With Arduino, you can design and build devices that interact with their environments. Arduino boards can read inputs—light on a sensor, an object near a sensor, a finger on a button, or a Twitter message—using their onboard microcontroller and convert them into an output—activating a motor, ringing an alarm, displaying information on an LCD, or publishing something online, for example. However, in order for you to create this action, you have to program the Arduino board, which I will explain later in this book. Many developers and electricians can easily create prototypes of products that make their ideas come to life using Arduino boards. This has enabled these amazing boards to gain considerable traction in both the hobby and professional markets.

A Brief History of Arduino

Many say that necessity is the mother of invention. Most of the greatest inventions in the history of mankind were in response to an existing problem or need that was lacking an easy solution. That is exactly what happened with the invention of Arduino. In the 20th century, it was very complex and expensive to prototype new electronics. This was an obstacle to many students in Italy who couldn't easily afford the BASIC Stamp microcontroller that was going for $100 at the time. This posed a great challenge to Massimo Banzi and his students at the Ivrea Interaction Design Institute.

So Banzi and his colleagues decided to come up with a solution to the complexity and increased costs of building electronics. Therefore in 2003, they worked on a project that had been started by one of their students and they successfully made an inexpensive and easier platform for building electronics. Hernando Barragán's wiring platform was his Master's thesis project. The goal of the project was to make simple, less expensive tools for creating digital projects using a non-engineering platform. The result was a wiring platform made from just three parts: an IDE, a microcontroller, and a printed circuit board. Banzi and his team developed the project further and added support for the less expensive ATmega8 microcontroller, which helped them hit their target price for the board that they later named Arduino.

Since that first board was built, lighter and cheaper versions have been distributed through the open-source community. And by May 2011, it is estimated that more than 300,000 Arduino boards had been commercially produced.

Features of Arduino

- Arduino allows you to load your own code into your Arduino IDE with a USB cable. You don't need an extra piece of hardware to load a new code into the board.
- Arduino is a cross-platform software. It can run on Windows, Mac OS, and Linux while other microcontroller systems run on Windows alone.
- Arduino only needs 5V to power up.
- You can control the board functions using its program (IDE).
- Arduino boards are able to read inputs using their onboard microcontroller and convert them into outputs.
- It is easy to create and upload codes using Arduino IDE.
- Arduino also provides a standard form factor that breaks the functions of the microcontroller down into more accessible packages.
- It is open-source in both hardware and software.
- The Arduino IDE uses a simplified version of C++ with syntax highlighting and other features that make it easier to learn how to program.

Advantages of Arduino

- **Open source and extensible *hardware***. The plans for Arduino boards are published under a Creative Commons license; this permits experienced circuit designers to build their own models based on Arduino. These models might make changes and/or improve upon the original design. Inexperienced users can also build the breadboard version of the module so as to understand how it works while saving some money.
- **It is cheap**. Compared to other microcontroller platforms, Arduino boards are relatively cheap. You can get a pre-assembled Arduino module for less than 40 USD. The least expensive ones are hand-assembled.
- **Open source and extensible *software***. Arduino also comes with an open-supply software system feature that permits experienced programmers to use the Arduino code with the prevailing programming language libraries, which may be extended and changed.
- **It is simple and easy to use**. Most beginners find using Arduino Software (IDE) very simple. It is also flexible enough for advanced users to take advantage of the benefits as well. Its processing programming environment allows students to familiarize themselves with how it works without any steep financial commitment. In general, Arduino is as user-friendly as it

gets and can be operated by anyone, from beginners to experts.

- **It is cross-platform**. Most microcontroller systems can only be used on Windows. Arduino's IDE is among the very few software that works on all kinds of operating systems. It works well on Linux, Windows, Macintosh, etc.
- **Wide variety.** The Arduino platform has many variations, thus giving you a chance to choose the one that best suits your project. If you're having space constraints, you can go for an Arduino Nano which is only 43.18mm by 18.54mm. If you need one with more memory space and processing power, Arduino Mega would be your best choice.

Everything has a good side and a bad side. As many advantages that Arduino has, it also has its downfalls:

- The board has a shield and libraries that make it hard to connect to the internet. It is not impossible, but it isn't easy.
- The Arduino IDE does not have a debugger; this makes it hard to find errors in long codes.
- Arduino is not optimized for any specific use. It is meant to fulfill the needs of multipurpose projects.
- As much as its user-friendliness is an advantage, it is also a disadvantage. If you use it on electrical projects,

it's unlikely you'll gain a comprehension of the AVR microcontrollers.

- The Arduino doesn't have a lot of processing power, so pretty much any majorly intensive task is out of the question. So, there can be scenarios where opting for a microprocessor, like Raspberry Pi, is a better option over a microcontroller.

Real-Time Applications of Arduino

- **Smart Home.** We can control home activities using Arduino boards. You may access control systems like motion sensors, outlet control, temperature sensors, garage door control, airflow control, etc.

- **Industries.** Arduino is used in many industries due to its easy programming environment, signal types, and easy adaptation to new setups. Arduino boards are the most flexible and affordable alternatives to the industrial devices used to control and monitor the functionality of small legacy industrial systems.
- **Traffic Signal Control**. Nowadays, Arduino is often used to control traffic lights. It can also be used in real-time to control systems with programmable timings, like pedestrian lighting.
- **Medical.** An Arduino board can be used to make a heartbeat monitor. This type of monitor counts the

number of heartbeats in one minute. It is designed in a way that a heartbeat sensor module is attached in a way that when you put a finger on the sensor, the heartbeat is detected. Arduino is also used to design medical equipment like thermometers and breathalyzers.

- **Laboratories**. Arduino provides a useful platform in laboratories for designing and learning circuit designing. The Arduino simulator prevents any damage from occurring in the lab. In addition to this, the students won't need to spend money on hardware. It also allows for faster circuit prototyping and no fuss with cabling at all. The Arduino-based, automated, slide-movement microscope is also a very cost-effective laboratory device.
- **Defense.** RADAR, Radio Detection and Ranging, is an Arduino technology that uses radio waves to detect the range, altitude, direction, and speed of objects. Radar has different sizes and performance specifications, and it can be used to control air traffic, long-range surveillance, and early warning systems in ships. It is also used in war.

Chapter One: Arduino Models

There are different types of Arduino boards that use different microcontrollers. These boards are distinguished by the different features that they possess. Some Arduino boards have more input and output pins than others, and some models are faster than others, have higher operation voltage, or opt for an embedded programming interface. Some can run directly from a 3.7V battery while others need at least 5V. However, all Arduino boards are programmed through the Arduino IDE. Let's take a close look at these boards.

Arduino UNO

Arduino UNO, also known as classic Arduino, is a great choice for your first Arduino board experience. It is the most commonly used board and has everything you need to get started. That's why it is the most recommended for beginners. The board has 14 digital input/output pins; 6 can be used as PWM output and 6 as analog inputs, a reset button, a power jack, a USB connection, and more. Uno runs on an ATMega328 chip and uses a USB, AC/DC adapter, or battery as a power source.

With the help of Arduino shields, you can exchange information over the internet using your Arduino board. You connect it to a computer using a USB or you can power it with an AC-to-DC adapter or battery, and you will be ready to go!

The board tolerates 12V power only. To avoid the risk of overheating, don't use higher currents than 12V. It also has a 5V pin that supports 5 volts of power and other lower voltages when running projects that require lower currents.

Specs

- 8-bit CPU
- 2KB SRAM
- 32 KB flash memory
- 1 KB EEPROM
- 16MHz clock speed
- Form factor is 2.1 inches by 2.7 inches rectangular board

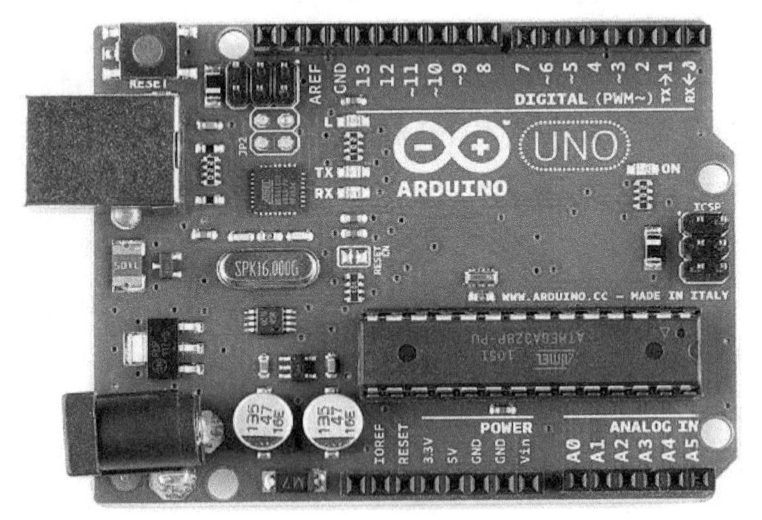

Advantages

- It has a simple circuitry that utilizes a small footprint; this makes it the perfect Arduino for smaller projects.
- It is widely available and accessible.

- It is the cheapest Arduino board going for $30 or less.
- There are many projects shared online by UNO users. This enables novice Arduino users to try out a variety of projects.

Disadvantages

- You can run out of pins, particularly if you fail to utilize an external integrated circuit
- It doesn't have a large memory; this keeps people from using it for special projects.

Arduino Mega

This is Arduino UNO's big brother. It is the next recommended board for beginners after UNO. It is suitable for bigger projects. The board itself has 54 digital input/output pins and 14 are used as PWM outputs while 16 are used as analog inputs, USB connection, a reset button, a power jack, and more. Just like Arduino UNO, it has everything needed to support the microcontroller. You only need to connect it to a computer using a USB or power it with an AC-to-DC adapter or battery and you will be ready to go.

Advantages of Arduino Mega

- It can hold a higher number of programs compared to Uno.
- Besides the massive number of input/output pins, Mega comes in two variations that could meet a specific developer's requirements even further. The first variation is faster due to its 32-bit ARM. It also offers more resources to support advanced projects and only runs at a 3.3V power. ADK is the second variation designed for Android phones. If you want to explore mobile computing, then this one is the best choice.
- It has a generous storage space and memory capacity for coding and running programs.
- It can support several projects without needing an external integrated circuit.

- There are a lot of projects online provided by individuals who have been using Mega for a long time.

Disadvantages

- There is a need for modifying codes. The guides shared for this Arduino always require users to make some slight changes to the codes depending on the number of pins.
- It is more expensive than the Arduino UNO.
- There are high chances of beginners damaging the board while in the middle of setting up a project.
- It is not as widely available as UNO. Therefore, it may be challenging to find it together with the accessories needed to execute a project, depending where you are purchasing it from.

Lily Pad Arduino

LilyPad was developed by Leah Buechley in 2006 as a wearable e-textile technology. The LilyPad board also has its own family of input, output, power, and sensor boards built specifically for e-textile. You can even wash them! It differs from all other models in shape. Unlike other models, which are rectangular in shape, LilyPad comes in a round shape with a flower-like pattern.

Red Board

The Red Board is programmable on a USB Mini-B cable using Arduino IDE. It can even be used on Windows 8 without changing the security settings. This board is more stable due to the USB/FTDI chip used. It is also completely flat on the back, making it easy to embed in your projects.

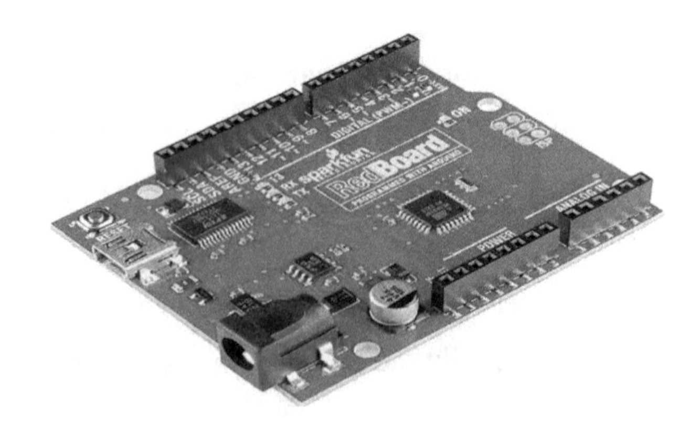

Arduino Leonardo

This is the first Arduino board to use one microcontroller with a built-in USB. This makes it cheaper and simpler. The board has code libraries as it handles the USB directly. This allows it to function as a computer keyboard or mouse.

Arduino Pro

Arduino Pro is mostly meant for experts and professional developers. It shares some features with the UNO, like power capacity and the lack of header pins. For connections to function, they must be soldered onto the board. Therefore, Arduino Pro requires expert or professional handling.

BLK
9 8 7 6 5 4 3 2 GND RST RXI TXO
GND VCC RXI TXO
Reset
Arduino Pro Mini
10 11 12 13 A0 A1 A2 A3 VCC RST GND RAW
GRN

Chapter Two: The Arduino Hardware

The Arduino board is comparable to a regular computer motherboard. Its parts work together in sending signals from input to output channels, power distribution, and executing coded functions. The parts of Arduino boards are located at different places depending on the models, but the majority of Arduinos have the same components. We are going to study the Arduino UNO because it is the most popular and commonly used board in the Arduino family.

1. **Reset Button** – It functions the same way as a gaming console's reset buttons. When you push it briefly, it connects to the reset pin and restarts the codes that have been uploaded to the board. This component is useful to people who use non-repetitive codes but want to test them multiple times.
2. **AREF** – This stands for "Analog Reference." Depending on the project they are building, users may or may not use this pin. It is used when you want to set an external reference voltage of 0-5 volts as the upper limit for the analog input pins.
3. **Ground Pins** – All Arduino boards have a few ground pins and all of them function the same. They all serve as a reference point in connecting components with varying voltage capacities. They set a common ground that prevents a high voltage current from flowing through a low voltage connection. Ground pins allow you to install a 12V part to a 5V Arduino. Ground pins are always found with analog and digital pin groups and their numbers vary from model to model.
4. **Digital Input and Output** – Digital pins are located on the topmost side of the board and lie across the analog pins. The number of these pins vary from model to model; Arduino UNO has 14 of them, for instance. They can either be arranged as input pins with the ability

to comprehend logic values or as output pins that can power a module.

5. **PWM** – This stands for Pulse-Width Modulation. These are the pins marked with the (~) symbol. PMW allows Arduino to carry out sophisticated circuitry control like fading an LED light through the simulation of an analog output.
6. **USB Connection** – Each Arduino board requires a connection to a power source. You can power an Arduino UNO using a USB cable connected to your computer or a wall power supply terminated in a barrel jack. Just like in flash drives, a USB connection distributes electricity throughout the board. The Arduino board USB port size is just the same as those on your computer. Not all Arduino boards have USB ports, however. So, if you prefer using a USB connection as a power gateway, check the power source online before purchasing an Arduino board. The USB connection is also used to load codes onto the board. You are required to write your code on your computer, then load it on the board the same way you transfer files.
7. **TX or RX** – TX means transmit while RX means receive. They appear in two places on the Arduino boards. One is at the digital pins 0 and 1 indicating the pins responsible for serial communication. The second one is located near the LEDs that indicate TX and RX.

The TX LEDs flash during the sending process of the data serial. The RX on the other hand flashes during the receiving process.

8. **ATmega Microcontroller** – This is the brain of an Arduino board. This is where the programs are stored. Each board has its own microcontroller, and the main integrated circuit on the Arduino board varies slightly from model to model. The microcontrollers are usually from the brand ATmega. It is important to know the integrated circuit of your board before loading a new program from the Arduino IDE.
9. **Power LED Indicator** – An Arduino board has one LED light that serves as a power indicator. This LED lights up when the board is connected to a power source. If it does not light up, then there is something wrong with the connection.
10. **Voltage Regulator** – You may not interact with the voltage regulator on your Arduino board. However, it is important to know that it exists, and that it is very useful. Just as the name suggests, the voltage regulator does exactly that — it controls the amount of voltage going onto the Arduino board. It turns away any extra voltage that might harm the circuit. Of course, it has limits; experts recommend not plugging an Arduino into a power source with over 20 volts.

11. **DC Power Barrel Jack** – Supplies your Arduino board with power. You can power your Arduino board directly from the AC main's power supply by connecting it to the barrel jack.
12. **3.3V Pin** – This pin supplies your projects with 3.3 volts of power.
13. **5V Pin** – This pin supplies your projects with 5 volts of power.
14. **Ground Pins** – See number three above.
15. **Analog Pins** – If you are viewing the board with the power jack on the lower left side, the set of analog pins is located at the lower right corner. These pins differ in number depending on the Arduino board model. Analog pins are used to convert signals from analog sensors to digital values.

Other Components

An Arduino board is just a single part of a project. You need to connect other components with it to ensure the project functions as expected. Apart from Arduino PCB, you will need to verify the following components and purchase them for your project:

- **Shields.** These are placed on top of the main Arduino board to extend its capabilities. You can usually purchase the shields together with Arduino PCB at the same shop. There are different types of shields available that work well and vary for each type of project. The most commonly used shields are:

- ❖ **Xbee**. This serves as a wireless communication gateway in between Arduino boards. It covers a distance of up to 100 feet when indoors and 300 feet when used in an outdoor space.
- ❖ **Motor Control**. This module lets users control and manipulate DC motors and read their encoders.
- ❖ **Custom shields.** Some developers prefer customizing their own shield that is best suited to their project. Developers can create their own shields by following the guidelines listed online.

- **Wire.** Wires are connectors that aid the flow of electricity or data transfer. We have two types of wire used in Arduino: the physical wire and the wire gauges. The physical wires are also divided into two categories: solid and stranded. Solid wires are ideal for projects when you don't need them to bend, as stranded wires have the tendency to bend excessively. However, they are still a good choice for appliance cords or audio and video output cables. Wire gauges are used together with breadboards, which support the installation of gauge wires.

- **Breadboard**. The breadboard resembles a small white board with many square holes. It is used for circuit construction and testing.
- **Capacitor.** This is a small component with two charging plates and an additional material that controls electricity discharge. It retains and releases the charge in a circuit connection.
- **Resistor**. A resistor is a must-have component on PCBs that resists the electricity flow, guaranteeing smooth electricity flow within the system. It protects the boards in instances of power fluctuations, which can affect the entire project.
- **Transistor**. This allows the flow of current from one point to another. Whether the third point is present or not, the current flow happens.
- **Diode**. A diode is a device that allows the unidirectional flow of electricity. We have several types of diodes, but LED, light-emitting diodes, and photodiodes (which detect light) are the most common.

Chapter Three: The Arduino Software

After learning the hardware part of Arduino, it is very important to learn its software, because complex coding is needed to generate the desired results in project development. Arduino software is an open-source program that is used as a platform to write the set of instructions that the Arduino needs to perform a particular action. Arduino uses software known as an IDE, Integrated Development Environment. This program is user-friendly and can be downloaded, installed on your computer, and used to write the codes that you need to load onto the Arduino board.

There are different versions of the Arduino IDE available on the market that are compatible with major operating systems. The latest version is the IDE 2.0 beta which is faster and more powerful than its predecessor, the 1.8.15 version. Arduino IDE version 2.0 has other amazing features besides the modern editor and a more responsive interface. It has autocompletion, a code navigator, and a live debugger.

Installation Process

First, you have to install the Arduino software on your computer before using the Arduino PCB. This is the general rule. The installation procedure is as follows:

Step 1. You Must Choose Your Arduino Board First.

Do some research and select your favorite board and a USB cable. Different Arduino models have their own types of compatible USB cables. You will need a standard USB if you are going to use Arduino UNO, Arduino Mega 2560, or Diecimila boards. However, if you are going to use Arduino Nano, you will need an A to Mini-B cable.

Step 2: Download Arduino IDE Software.

There are different versions of Arduino IDE available on the download page of the official Arduino website. Select and download the one that is compatible with your operating system—Windows, IOS, or Linux. Unzip the file once it is done downloading, and then extract and install the downloaded program.

Step 3: Power Up Your Board.

Once the program is installed, plug the board into the computer using the USB cable. Some Arduino boards like UNO, Mega, and Nano automatically connect from the USB connection to the computer or another external power supply. However, some models, like Arduino Diecimila, require the proper configuration to draw power from the USB connection. You need to select the power source using a jumper; ensure that the jumper is on the two pins closest to the USB port, then connect the Arduino board to your computer using the USB cable. Remember, the power LED should light up.

Step 4: Install Arduino Drivers.

Your computer's operating system has to install Arduino's driver before it starts receiving codes. Arduino boards work like a plug-and-play system. Once a new device is plugged in, the operating system detects it and installs its drivers automatically. However, in some circumstances, this procedure may fail and require you to configure the driver manually.

To install the drivers manually:

1. Open Device Manager and search for Ports (COM & LPT).
2. You will find your Arduino listed under this group as "Arduino (Model) (COMxx)."
3. If it's not listed, go to "Other Devices" and look for "Unknown Device." This means that the newly plugged-in device was detected but was not identified correctly due to the lack of pre-installed drivers.
4. Double click on the Arduino model and select "Update Driver Software." This will direct you to another dialog box.
5. Select "Browse my computer for driver software."
6. Look for the Arduino installer and select the "Drivers" folder.

7. Select "Arduino.inf" to install.

However, there are instances when "Arduino.inf" is missing. This is more frequent in the Arduino IDE's older versions. If this is the case for you, look for the driver that has the Arduino's model name. For example, if you are using the UNO model, search for the file "Arduino UNO.inf" and select it to install.

Another thing that may also interfere with the installation process is a difference in the operating system. The process is instant with newer operating systems unlike with their predecessors.

The device should display the "Add New Hardware" dialog box when plugged in. Select "Install from a list or specified location (Advanced)." Click next to be directed to the next prompts, and then check the "Search for the best driver in these locations" box—and uncheck "Search removable media." Also, select the "Include this location in the search" option and search for the drivers /FTDI in the USB Drivers directory.

Visit the FTDI website and download the newer versions of the driver as the available drivers may be outdated. Click next. The system will report finding a "USB Serial Converter." Click on it and finish the installation process. You should be able to find the newly installed hardware under Ports (COM & LPT).

Step 5: Open the Arduino Software to See Sample Codes.

Arduino IDE comes with preset codes that can be used as references for beginners. Upon starting the program, you can either create a new project or open an existing one. Click File > Examples > Basics > Blink to open the blink project examples in the program. You will see the code together with the description of what the code should do for the project. The blink project code indicates that the command will turn a LED on and off with some delay time. You can select any project from the list to practice, and if you want to create a new project, select File > New.

Step 6: Load Example Codes to Arduino.

You must select the correct Arduino board name that matches with the board connected to your computer to avoid errors while uploading your code. To do this:

1. Go to Tools > Board
2. Check the box with your Arduino model
3. Select a port that corresponds to your Arduino board
4. Open the menu and look for the available ports if you are not sure which is the right port for your board. Disconnect the board then open the menu again. The port that is missing after reopening the menu is the one

assigned to your board. Reconnect the board and select that port.

5. Once you've selected the port, click "Upload" to load the programmed code.
6. You should see a light flashing on the board. This tells you that the codes are being processed and uploaded.
7. Your computer will then display a dialogue box that says, "Done uploading." This shows that the code has been uploaded successfully.

Step 7: Observe the Effects.

Once you are done uploading, wait for a few seconds and you should see the board's LED light blinking!

Chapter Four: Coding Fundamentals

The basic structure of Arduino programming runs in at least two parts and is fairly simple. These parts enclose blocks of statements. Here is the structure.

```
void setup()
{
statements;
}
void loop()
{
statements;
}
```

Both the setup() and loop() functions are required for the program to work. Setup() is the preparation while loop() is the execution.

Arduino Functions

A function is a line of code used to define a task. A function executes the task as described in the code when it is loaded. Functions allow programmers to divide a specific code into segments with each segment performing a specific task. You can even use a single function to perform a task several times throughout the length of a program.

Function Declaration

A function is declared as follows:

```
int addNumbers(int y, int z)

{

int sum;

sum = y + z;

return sum;

}
```

Function Return Data Type

This is the first thing to declare in a function. Returned data type refers to the value returned after the code has been executed. If there is a value to be returned, then the function should have "int" for an integer. And if there is no value to be returned then it should have "void" in place of "int".

Function Name

After declaring the data type, the next thing is declaring the function name. A function name refers to the action or task to be done in the code. For example, the function name in this code is “addNumbers”. Naming functions is done the same way as naming variables. Here is the convention:

- You may use alphanumeric characters and an underscore (_)
- Function names may not start with a number
- Don’t use a name that is the same as the language keyword or existing function

Function Parameters

Parameters refer to the special variables used to pass data onto a function. In other words, it is the value of a function inherited. In our example above, the parameters are int y and int z.

Return Statement

This is the type of data that matches the declaration. A return statement in any code has the word “return” in it. That's why it is very easy to recognize the statement in a code. In our example above, the return statement is “Return sum;”.

Advantages of Using Functions

- Functions increase the readability of the code
- Functions reduce the chance of errors occurring
- Functions help you avoid statement or code repetitions
- Functions make the program compact and small

- Functions help programmers conceive and organize the program
- Functions enable you to divide a complex code or program into a simpler one
- Functions aid developers in spotting their needed codes immediately
- Functions makes the modification of programs easier

Main Functions

- **setup().** This function is called on at the beginning of the program and runs only once after the initial startup or reset. It is used to set pinMode or initialize serial communication.
- **loop().** The loop function includes code that is to be executed continuously. It reads inputs and then triggers output, over and over again. This function requires the microcontroller to repeat a function. You have to set a condition that stops the loop, or power off the Arduino board to stop it. This function is the core of all Arduino programs.

Arduino I/O functions

- **pinMode(pin, mode)**. This function is used to configure a specified pin to behave either as an input (INPUT), input with a pull-up resistor (INPUT_PULLUP), or an output (OUTPUT). Pins configured as INPUT are said to be in a high-impedance state.

- **digitalRead(pin)**. This function is used to read the value from a specified digital pin with the result being either HIGH or LOW. There are two ways a pin can be defined: a variable or a constant. Arduino UNO board, for example, has 14 digital pins numbered 0 to 13.
- **digitalWrite(pin, value).** This function outputs either logic level HIGH or LOW at a specified digital pin. The pin can be specified as either a variable or constant from 0-13 if you are using the Arduino UNO model.
- **analogRead(pin).** This function works on analog pins 0-5 only. It is used to read the value from a specified analog pin with a 10-bit resolution. The value can be specified as either a variable or a constant and ranges from 0 to 1023. *Note:* Unlike digital pins, analog pins don't need to be declared first as INPUT or OUTPUT.
- **analogWrite(pin, value).** This function outputs a pseudo-analog value using a hardware-enabled, pulse-width modulation to a pin marked PMW. The resulting integer value can be a variable or constant ranging from 0 to 255.

Time functions

- **delay(ms).** This function is used when you want to pause a program for a specified amount of time in milliseconds.
- **millis().** This function is used to determine the number of milliseconds that pass with each function on the Arduino board.

Other Functions

- **randomSeed(seed).** This function is used to set a value, or seed, as the starting point for the random() function. It allows you to put a variable, constant, or other function into the random function, thus generating more random numbers as Arduino can't create a truly random number.
- **random(min, max).** This function is used when you want to return pseudo-random numbers with a range specified between a determined min and max value. Remember to insert the randomSeed() function first before inserting this function.
- **Serial.begin(rate).** This function opens a serial port and sets its baud rate for serial-data transmission. The standard baud rate for communicating with the computer is 9600. However, other speeds are supported as well. *Note:* You can't use digital pins 0 (RX) and 1 (TX) at the same time as serial communication.

- **Serial.println(data).** This function is used to print data to the serial port, then carry out an automatic carriage and line feed.

SYNTAX

- **; (semicolon).** This is used to end a statement. It functions the same as period in the English language. Make sure that the statement closed by the semicolon is complete for the code to function properly. Forgetting to end a statement with a semicolon will result in a compiler error.
- **{} (curly braces).** These are used to determine where the function and statement blocks begin and where they end. To avoid compiler errors, if you insert an opening curly brace, you must follow it with a closing curly brace. This keeps the braces balanced, which is vital to getting your program working.
- **// (single-line comment).** This code should be used at the beginning of a comment that reminds you or tells others something about how your code functions. The comment should take up one line only. This line, however, does not transfer to the microcontroller's processor; it will live in the code and act as a reference to you and anyone reading the code manually.

- /* */ **(multi-line comment).** This type of comment spans more than one line and it is opened by inserting /*. It cannot contain another multi-line comment, but it can contain a single line comment. Make sure that you close the comment with */. If you fail to close it, all of your code following it will be considered a comment and will not be implemented.
- **#define.** This is used when you want to define a certain variable as a constant value. It gives a sort of shorthand name for that value. This helps in conserving space as defined variables don't take up memory space on the chip. The compiler replaces any instance of the constant as the value that is used to define it once the code is compiled. The #define statement does *not* require a semicolon at the end.
- **#include.** This is used when you want to include other libraries in your sketch that would not otherwise be included. This includes other words and coding languages like AVR C libraries. Don't add the semicolon at the end of this statement or you will create an error. Exclude it the way you would do in **#define a statement**.

Control Structures

Control structures tell us how an input will be received. They determine how your data will be read and compiled. Popular control structures in Arduino programming include:

- **If statements.** If statements are used to test whether a certain condition has been met. This links an input to an output. If the condition is met, a specific output or response of the microcontroller occurs. If the condition is not met, the program skips over this.
- **If . . . else statements.** This statement works like the "if" conditional, but it allows you to create an "either-or" reaction. In other words, it specifies another action that the microcontroller will take if the condition for the first action is not met. This enables you to perform two different actions in two different circumstances using one piece of code.
- **For loop.** This statement is used when you intend to repeat a block of statements enclosed in curly braces a specified number of times. To increment and terminate the loop, use the increment counter. The initialization of a local variable, or increment counter, happens first and only once. The following condition is tested each time throughout the loop until it becomes false.

- **While loop.** This loop continues infinitely until the expression inside the parenthesis becomes false. This means that it performs a certain function until a parameter is met and the condition becomes false. You have to change the tested variable for the while loop to exit. You may make changes to your code like increment variables or external conditions, like testing a sensor.
- **Do . . . while loop**. This loop works in the same manner as the while loop, but it tests the condition at the end of the function rather than at the beginning as it does with the while loop, so it always runs at least once.
- **Break.** This code acts as an emergency exit of sorts from a function of the microcontroller. It is used when you want to exit a do, for, or while loop without going through the normal loop condition. It is also used to exit from a switch statement.
- **Return.** This is a way of getting a value back from a function. It is used at the end of a function to get back the value for which the function was called for.
- **Goto.** This piece of code transfers the flow of the program to a labeled point in the code. It instructs the microcontroller to move to another place within the coded program. You can go to any part of the code if a certain condition is met. Goto can be used to create infinite loops, but its use is generally discouraged by C language programmers.

Chapter Five: Arduino Data Types

The programming environment for Arduino is more like that of C++. It defines a number of different data types that simplify the coding process. A data type is an attribute of data used for declaring functions and variables. A variable's type determines its storage space and how the bit pattern stored is interpreted. Below are the data types used in Arduino:

Note: *Signed* variables can represent both negative and positive numbers while *unsigned* variables only represent zero and positive numbers.

- **Void.** Void is a keyword used in function declaration only. It refers to a data type that has no value. It is used when you don't want to return any value from calling the function.

- **Boolean.** This is a simple logical "true or false." Each Boolean variable occupies a memory of 8-bits.

- **Int.** This stands for integer. This data type is considered the major storage for whole numbers. It occupies a memory of 2 bytes, which translates to a range of values from -32768 to 32767. However, the size varies from board to board. On some boards like Arduino Due, the int occupies a memory of 4 bytes with values ranging from -2,147,483,648 to 2,147,483,647.

- **Unsigned int.** This is the same as integers. The only difference is that they only represent positive numbers yielding a range of 0 to 65,535 for the 2-byte integer storage boards, and a range of 0 to 4,294,967,295 for boards like Due that have an integer memory of 4 bytes (32 bit).
- **Byte.** It represents 8-bit, unsigned, whole numbers that range from 0 to 255.
- **Float.** This data type is used to represent floating-point numbers. It stores 32-bit, signed numbers that have decimal points and range from -3.4028235E+38 to 3.4028235E+38. Floating point numbers have a greater resolution than integers. However, the Arduino's floating point isn't native; for it to work, the compiler has to jump through hoops. You are advised to avoid it if you can.
- **Word.** This represents a 16-bit, unsigned number ranging from 0 to 65535.
- **Long.** This data type represents extended-size, signed whole numbers. They are stored in 32-bit and range from -2,147,483,648 to 2,147,483,647.
- **Unsigned long**. This data type represents extended-size, non-negative integers. They occupy a storage of 32 bits and range from 0 to 4,294,967,295. It is commonly

used to store the results of the millis() function and returns the number of milliseconds that the current code has been running.

- **Short**. This is an integer data type that stores 2 bytes. The numbers range from -32,768 to 32,767.
- **Char.** This data type represents 8-bit, signed numbers ranging from -128 to 127. The compiler sometimes tries to analyze these numbers as characters, which often leads to unanticipated outcomes.
- **Unsigned char**. This is the same as byte; for clarity reasons, just use "byte" instead of this when possible.
- **Double.** This data type is exactly the same as float but with no gain in precision. A double-precision, floating-point number occupies 4 bytes on the UNO and other ATMEGA based boards. It occupies a storage space of 64-bits on the Arduino Due.

Chapter Six: Variables and Constants

Variables

Variables are storage places for numerical data that the program plans to use at a later time. It consists of a type, name, and value. Variables can be continually changed as opposed to constants whose values never change. The code syntax is:

Type Variable = Value

Example:

int pin = 7;

- **int** is the data type
- pin is the variable name
- 7 is the value initialized.

The data type **int** is used to create a variable named **pin** that stores the value 7.

How to Change Variable Value in Arduino

In Arduino, the variable value can be changed using the assignment operator "=". However, before you assign a value to your variable, you need to declare it first to avoid errors. For example, if you directly specify the value as: pin=8; you will get an error as that pin has not been declared. You can easily change a variable by copying its value to another variable.

Example:

```
void setup()
    {
    Serial.begin(9600);
    int pinLED = 8;
    Serial.println(pinLED); // will print value of 8
    int pin1 = pinLED;
    pinLED = 13;
     Serial.println(pinLED); // value is now changed
     // now, will print value 13
    }
```

Variable Scope

Variables in Arduino programming have a property called scope. A scope is a region of a program. It refers to the places or the number of ways that variables can be declared. There are two ways in which variables can be declared: local and global.

Local Variables

Local variables are declared inside a function or block. These variables have a scope only within the function and can only be used by statements that lie within that function.

Example:

```
void setup()
{
int pin = 14; // This is a local-variable declaration
```

```
pinMode(pin, OUTPUT);
 digitalWrite(pin, High);
}
```

Global Variables

Global variables are defined outside the setup() and loop() function. The variables hold their value throughout the program and can be accessed anywhere in the program.

Example:

```
int pin = 13; // This is a global-variable declaration
 void setup()
{
pinMode(pin, OUTPUT);
}
void loop()
 {
digitalWrite(pin, High)
 }
```

Advantages of Variables

- You can use them several times in a program.
- They can represent different data types.
- Variables increase the flexibility of the program.

- You can easily modify them by changing their values.
- You can specify any name for a variable.

Constants

In Arduino programming, constants are predefined expressions. Constants are used to make the programs easy to read. The constants in Arduino are grouped as:

- **True or false.** The true/false constant is the Boolean constant that is used to define logic levels. False is defined as 0 while true is defined as 1. However, true can also be anything else except 0. In Boolean language, any integer that is non-zero is determined as true. Therefore, -15 and -200 are also defined as true. The true/false constants are typed in lowercase, unlike the other constants.

- **HIGH/LOW.** These constants are used when defining pin levels as either HIGH or LOW. They are used when reading or writing digital pins. The HIGH value is provided by two types of voltage pins: 5V pins and 3V or 3.3V pins. HIGH is also defined as logic level 1 or ON. On the other hand, LOW is defined as logic level 0, OFF, or 0 volts. *Example:* digitalWrite(13, HIGH);

- **INPUT/OUTPUT.** In Arduino, we use the pinMode() function to configure pins as INPUT or OUTPUT. *Example:* pinMode(13, OUTPUT);

- **LED-_BUILTIN Constant.** Most Arduino boards have a built-in LED connected in series with a resistor. The LED-_BUILTIN constant defines the number of the pin that the on-board LED is connected to. Most Arduino boards have this LED connected to digital pin number 13.

Chapter Seven: Arduino Operators

Operators play a crucial role in every programming concept. In Arduino programming, operators are widely used from basic to advanced levels. An operator is a character that determines the action that the compiler needs to take to solve a problem. The types of operators that are used in Arduino programming include:

1. Arithmetic Operators

Arithmetic operators are responsible for performing mathematical operations like addition, subtraction, and multiplication. They are listed in the table below.

Note: In the examples given in the tables, we assume that the variable A holds a value of 10 while B holds a value of 20.

Operator Name	**Symbol**	**Function**	**Example**
Assignment	=	It is used to assign the value to the right side of the equal sign to the variable on the left side.	A=10

Addition	+	This is used when you want to add two operands.	Suppose you want to add A and B: A+B will give you 30.
Modulo	%	This is used to calculate the remainder after dividing two numbers.	B%A will give you 0.
Division	/	This is used when you want to divide two operands.	B/A will give you 2.
Multiplication	*	This is used when you want to multiply two.	A*B will return 200.
Subtraction	-	This is used to calculate the	B-A will give you 10.

		difference between two operands	

2. Comparison Operators

Comparison operators are used to compare the value of two operands. They return a Boolean value of true or false after the comparison.

Note: In the examples given in the table below, we assume that the variable A holds a value of 10 while B holds a value of 20.

Operator Name	**Symbol**	**Function**	**Example**
Equal to	==	This is used when you want to check whether the values of two operands are equal or not; if they are, then the condition is satisfied and it becomes true.	The statement (A == B) is not true.

Not equal to	!=	This is used when you want to check whether the values of two operands are equal or not, if they are not then the condition is satisfied and it becomes true.	The statement (A != B) is true.
Greater than	>	This is used when you want to check whether the operand on the left side is greater than the operand on the right side. The statement becomes true if the condition is satisfied.	The statement (A > B) is not true.
Less than	<	This is used when you want to check whether the value on the left side of the statements is less than that on the right side. The statement becomes true if the condition is satisfied.	The statement (A < B) is true.

Less than or equal to	<=	This is used when you want to check whether the value of the left operand is less than or equal to the value of the right operand. The statement becomes true if the condition is satisfied.	The statement (A < = B) is true.
Greater than or equal to	>=	This is used when you want to check whether the value of the left operand is greater than or equal to the value of the right operand. The statement becomes true if the condition is satisfied.	The statement (A >= B) is not true.

3. The Boolean Operators

Boolean operators help make decisions depending on the condition in instances where you have to combine the results of two or more conditions. They are also known as logical operators. They include:

Note: In examples given in the tables, we assume that the variable A holds a value of 10 while B holds a value of 20.

<table>
<tr><th>Operator Name</th><th>Symbol</th><th>Function</th><th>Example</th></tr>
<tr><td>Logical AND</td><td>&&</td><td>It returns a true condition result if both the operands in the condition are true.</td><td>(A != B && A < B) is true.</td></tr>
<tr><td>Logical OR</td><td>||</td><td>It returns a true condition result if either of the variables in the condition is true.</td><td>The statement (A < B || A > B) is true.</td></tr>
<tr><td>Logical NOT</td><td>!</td><td>It is used to determine the truth and falsity of an operation. If the statement is true,</td><td>! (A != B && A < B) is false.</td></tr>
</table>

		then this operator returns false.	

4. **Bitwise Operators**

Bitwise operators perform operations at the binary level and give the result in a decimal representation. They include:

Note: In these examples, we assume that A holds a value of 60 and variable B holds a value of 13.

Operator Name	**Symbol**	**Function**	**Example**
Bitwise AND	&	It is used to compare the first bit of operand to the second one. It returns 1 if both bits are 1, and 0 if not.	The condition (A & B) will give 12 whose binary form is 0000 1100.

Bitwise OR	|	This is used to compare two bits and returns 1 if either or both of the bits are 1, and it returns 0 if both bits are 0.	The condition (A | B) will give 61 whose binary form is 0011 1101.
Bitwise XOR	^	. It is used to compare two bits and returns 1 if the bits are different and 0 if they are not.	The condition (A ^ B) will give 49 whose binary form is 0011 0001.
Bitwise NOT	~	This is complementary and it is used to invert all of the bits of the operand.	The condition (~A) will give -60 whose binary digit is 1100 0011.
Shift Left	<<	This moves the bits to the left, discards the far-left bit, and assigns the	The condition A << 2 will give 240 whose

		rightmost bit a value of 0. Each move to the left effectively multiplies the left operand by 2	binary form is 1111 0000.
Shift Right	>>	Just as the name suggests, it is used to move the bit pattern in an expression to the right. Every move to the right effectively divides the left operand in half.	The condition A >> 2 will give 15 whose binary digit is 0000 1111.

5. Compound Operators

Note: In the examples given in the table below, we assume that the variable C holds a value of 20 while D holds a value of 30.

Operator Name	**Symbol**	**Function**	**Example**
Increment	++	This increases the operand value by 1.	C++ will give 21.
Decrement	—	This decreases the operand value by 1.	C-- will give 19.
Compound Addition	+=	This adds the right operand to the left operand and then assigns the results to the left operand.	D += C is equivalent to D = D+ C.
Compound Subtraction	-=	This subtracts the right operand from the left operand and then assigns the results to the left operand.	D -= C is equivalent to D = D - C.

Compound Multiplication	*=	This multiplies the right operand with the left operand and then assigns the results to the left operand.	D*= C is equivalent to D = D* C.
Compound Division	/=	This divides the left operand with the right operand and then assigns the results to the left operand.	D /= C is equivalent to D = D / C.
compound modulo	%=	It is used to determine the remainder after dividing two operands.	D %= C is equivalent to D = D % C.
Compound Bitwise OR	|=	This takes the Bitwise OR of the right operand with the left operand and then assigns the	C |= 2 is same as C = C | 2.

		results to the left operand	
Compound Bitwise AND	&=	This takes the Bitwise AND of the right operand with the left operand and then assigns the results to the left operand.	C &= 2 is same as C = C & 2.

Chapter Eight: Arduino Projects

Arduino is an all-encompassing device that enables you to complete virtually any project. Some people, especially beginners, are tempted to write a sketch for their project ideas immediately after starting their first projects. But it is important to follow through with some basic preparatory steps before you start writing your own code. You should know that the Arduino board does not read your mind; it requires precise instructions, and these instructions must be correct. Even though the instructions may be executed error-free, overlooking even a minor detail may not return the results you expected.

Whether it is a simple project that emulates the traffic lights or a complex, automated project, a detailed plan is the foundation of success in building any code. Below are the basic steps to take when designing your Arduino projects:

1. **Define your project goal.** Determine what you want to achieve with your project.

2. **Write your algorithm.** An algorithm is a set of instructions to follow in order to complete a specific task. It lists what you want to accomplish at the end of your project and how to do it. Your algorithm lists the steps to be followed to achieve your project's goal.

3. **Select your hardware.** Ensure that you have all the hardware that needs to be connected to the Arduino and determine how to set it up correctly.

4. **Wire it up**. Connect your hardware, circuitry, and any other items to the Arduino board. Ensure that everything is where it should be because if you fail to connect everything correctly, your project will not work.

5. **Write your sketch.** Pay attention to every detail when writing your sketch. Create your initial program that instructs the Arduino what to do. Make sure that all your variables and functions are declared properly.

6. **Test and debug.** Before you upload your code to the Arduino board, test and check for any errors. Identify the cause of any error that may exist, be it hardware-related or in the algorithm. Remove all the identified errors and test it again.

Project 1: Blinking LED

This is one of the simplest projects you can do with an Arduino to see the physical output and performance of your Arduino board. It is very basic and any enthusiastic developer or individual who wants to start learning Arduino can succeed with this one. This program makes an LED connected to the board blink within a particular time interval. It is as simple as turning the lights on and off.

Required Hardware

- Arduino UNO
- Breadboard
- LED
- Resistor
- Jumper Wires

The Algorithm

- Turn the LED on
- Wait for two seconds
- Turn the LED off
- Wait for two seconds
- Do it repeatedly

Procedure

Step 1: Wire the circuit and components. Connect the LED to a digital output pin on the Arduino. Let the digital pin 7 on your board go to a spot on your breadboard and then your resistor. Connect the LED to the remaining side of the resistor. Remember, LEDs are polarized, so you should be keen on ensuring that the right leg goes to the right place on the resistor. Connect the positive leg of the LED to the resistor and run a jumper wire from the ground lead to a pin labeled GND on your Arduino board.

Step 2: Make the Arduino program. Write the code. The Arduino board can be programmed to do almost anything you can think of. The code for this project is quite simple.

Begin by declaring and naming your variable. In this project, we are going to assign a name to pin 7 so that we know what we are controlling. Since we are controlling the LED, we will assign the name led to pin 7. So, write:

int led = 7;

This will assign the integer 7 the name "led." So, Arduino will be interpreting led as 7 anytime you write led in your code. After you've declared your variable, write this:

void setup()

void loop()

This means that the code within the void setup section is run when you boot up or reset your Arduino. After that, the code in the void loop sections gets run repeatedly until the Arduino is disconnected from power.

Now, you want to write a line of code that instructs the Arduino to let it know that it should treat pin 7, or the led, as an output. An output pin is assigned either HIGH or LOW to indicate if it is either ON or OFF. So you will need to write this line after the void setup():

pinMode(led, OUTPUT);

This built-in function tells the Arduino that the led is the output. Remember that it is very important to end each line in a semicolon. Don't forget it. It will help you avoid unnecessary compiler errors.

Next, we need a line of code for the actual controlling of the LED. So after the void loop(), write this:

digitalWrite(led, HIGH);

This commands or sets pin 7 asHIGH, meaning that it is outputting volts. This code will light up the LED if you run it. You may try if you want now to make sure it's working alright.

Now, remember our goal is to have the LED turned on and off. So, we will have to set the waiting time before it is switched on and off. Therefore, on the next line write:

delay(2000);

This will pause the Arduino, or rather the LED, for two seconds. You can make it one second, half a second or anything that you want. But if you try running the code, it will still not blink. Write the following line of code on the line after that:

digitalWrite(led, LOW);

This will turn your LED off after the two seconds you set in the delay code line. However, if you run the code, you will notice that the LED still doesn't blink. Why? Is there something wrong in our codes up there? No. Our code is not yet complete, keeping in mind what the void loop function does.

This means that it loops immediately until it reaches the line that turns the LED off. In other words, there isn't any time for it to keep the LED off. The solution to this is to add another delay-code line. So, write this under the digitalWrite(led, LOW);:

delay(2000);

The Final Code

```
int led = 7;
void setup()
 {
pinMode(led, OUTPUT);
}
void loop()
 {
digitalWrite(led, HIGH); // turn the LED on
delay(2000); // wait for two seconds (values are given in
milliseconds)
digitalWrite(led, LOW); // makes the voltage low,
turning off the LED
delay(2000); // wait for two seconds before going back
```

```
}
```

Once you run this code, you should see a blinking LED! The led turns on for two seconds and off for another two seconds.

Project 2. Traffic Light Controller

This is a fun, simple project that uses an Arduino board and some LEDs to replicate traffic lights.

Hardware required

- Arduino UNO board
- Jumper wires
- Breadboard
- Red, Yellow, and Green LED lights
- Arduino USB 2.0 Cable
- Resistors

Procedure

Step 1: Power your breadboard. Connect your jumper wire to the board such that one end of the wire goes into GND while the other end goes to the pin on the far-right top of the breadboard.

Step 2: Add the LEDs. One end of the resistor should go in the same column with your jumper wires and the other end to any row on the breadboard. The same row should hold your LEDs. The short end of your LEDs goes to the side where the resistors are, while the other end goes to the other side of the breadboard. Note: You must connect the LEDs correctly or else the project will not work.

Step 3: Complete the circuit. Place another jumper wire on the row that has the LEDs. This is where the wires will go:

- Green LED connects to pin 8, on the digital PWM section
- Yellow LED connects to pin 9, on the digital PWM section
- Red LED connects to pin 10, on the digital PWM section

This is how your circuit should look like after the connection:

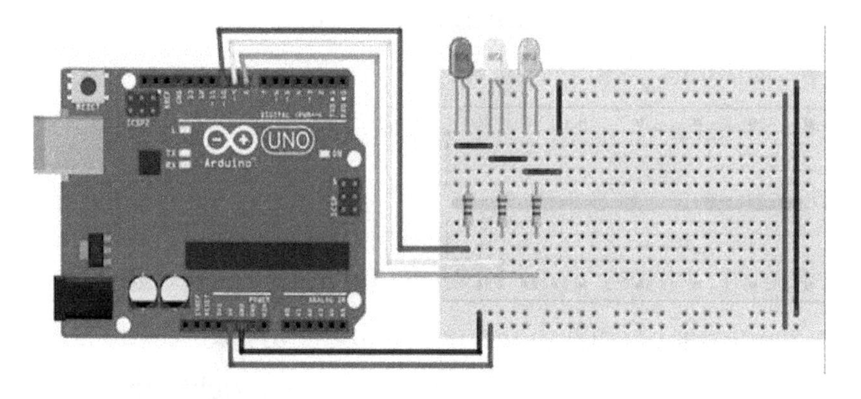

Coding for Arduino Traffic-Light Controller

- First, you will have to declare the variables so that you address the lights by name rather than a pin number. For example, the GREEN variable in our project represents the pin the green LED is connected to.
- Next, add the setup function that configures the LEDs to be OUTPUTs. Here you may refer to the pins by names since you have already defined your variables.

- The loop function creates a loop that the program will run through such that any time you call a function, a light turns on, and you set a delay so that it changes after a period of time lapses.
- Create a function for each LED. For example in the code below, the **greenlight()** function should turn on the green LED while turning off the yellow and red LEDs.

The Final Code:

```
// variables
int greedledPin = 8; // the pin number the green LED is
connected to
int yellowledPin= 9; // the pin number the yellow LED is
connected to
int redledPin = 10;   // the pin number the red LED is
connected to


void setup()
{
 pinMode(greenledPin, OUTPUT); // define greenledPin
as an output
 pinMode(yellowledPin, OUTPUT); // define
yellowledPin as an output
 pinMode(redledPin, OUTPUT);    // define redledPin
as an output
}
```

```
void loop()
{
  green_light();
  delay(greenledPin, 5000); // the green LED will stay
for five seconds
  yellow_light();
  delay(yelloledPin, 5000); // the yellow LED will stay
for five seconds
  red_light();
  delay(redledPin, 5000); // the red LED will stay for five
seconds
}
void green_light()
{
  digitalWrite(greenledPin, HIGH); // turns on the green
LED
  digitalWrite(yellowledPin, LOW); // the yellow LED is
turned off
  digitalWrite(redledPin, LOW);     // the red LED is
turned off
}
void yellow_light()
{
  digitalWrite(greenledPin, LOW);  // the green LED is
turned off
```

```
  digitalWrite(yellowledPin, HIGH); // the yellow LED
turns on
  digitalWrite(redledPin, LOW);       // the red LED is
turned off
}
void red_light()
{
  digitalWrite(greenledPin, LOW);  // the green LED is
turned off
  digitalWrite(yellowledPin, LOW); // the yellow LED
turned off
  digitalWrite(redledPin, HIGH);    // the red LED turns
on
}
```

Once you are done writing your code, click the verify button to test it before uploading it to the Arduino. The lights should start blinking in the pattern defined in the function calls and the delays.

Project 3: Fading LED

This project demonstrates the use of the analogWrite() function to fade an LED on and off. Remember, this function has nothing to do with analog pins on the Arduino boards.

Most Arduino boards have 5 pins marked with 'PWM' next to the pin number. Some boards, however, have these pins marked with the "~" symbol. You can program these pins to quickly modify the power being sent their way. We refer to this technique as Pulse With Modulation (PWM). You can use this technique to turn an LED connected to your board on and off rapidly with different ratios in between to create a fading effect.

Hardware required

- Arduino UNO board
- Breadboard
- One LED of any color
- 220 Ohm resistor
- Two jumper wires

Procedure

Step 1: Wire up the circuit and components. Connect the longer leg, which is the anode or positive side of the LED, to digital output pin 5 on your board through the resistor. Take the shorter leg of the LED and insert it directly into the GND pin.

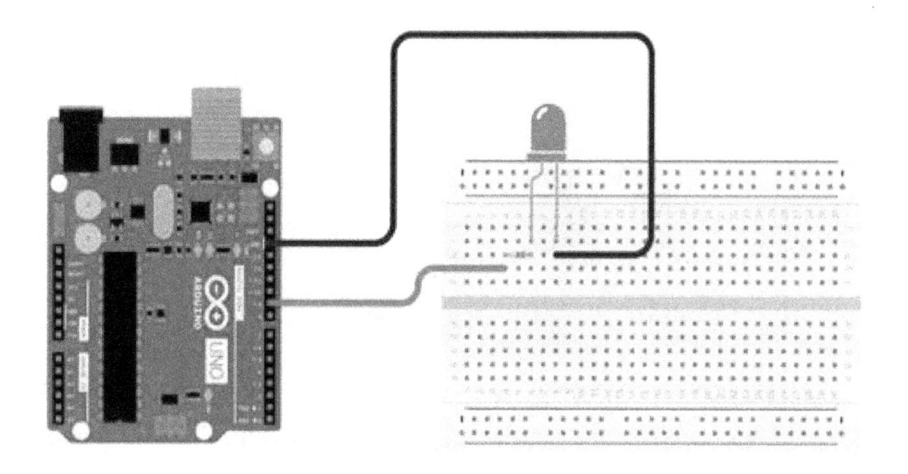

Step 2: Write your Code. As usual, the first thing we do when writing our code is declare our variables. In our code, we are going to declare three variables, the pin number, the current brightness of the LED, and the rate at which the LED will brighten and fade.

The next thing is to tell the Arduino that pin 5 is going to be an output using the pinMode( ) function in the setup( ) routine. By now, you should know that the setup() functions run only once. Therefore, the code within the curly braces under setup() will be executed only once. The real action occurs in the loop().

The next step involves writing a line of code for the actual controlling of the LED. And here, we are going to use the analogWrite() function. Remember that this function takes two arguments: one tells the Arduino the pin number to write to, and two indicates the value of PWM to write.

Basically, Pulse Width Modulation (PWM) adjusts the power output of the LED. So, you can regulate the amount of power—or rather brightness of your LED. Just tell your Arduino the pin to modulate and the amount of power to be applied using the analogWrite() function. The scale ranges from 0 to 255 with 0 being the minimum and 255 the maximum.

As per our code below, the first thing we've done in the loop is that we've written a value to pin 5 where we have our LED connected and we've set the value to be 255. This will keep our LED bright to start with.

Things to Note About the analogWrite() Function

- It has got nothing to do with analog pins
- On most Arduino boards, it can be used with pins 3, 5, 6, 9, 10, and 11
- It adjusts power output using Pulse Width Modulation (PWM)
- It takes two arguments: pin number and value

The next line of code has the delay time. This indicates the time the LED pauses to enable you to see the dimming effect.

We will then write this code: brightness = brightness - fadeAmount; to dim the LED. This instructs the Arduino to take the current brightness value and subtract the fadeAmount from it and then save the new value back to the brightness variable.

Our brightness variable will now hold a value of 252, thus reducing the intensity.

This will in turn make our LED dim. This is going to repeat and every time the loop runs, we subtract 3 from our brightness variable until we have a very dim LED. However, if this is to continue, the brightness variable will quickly drop to 0. Therefore, we need to set a condition that controls this, so that the LED brightens again and turns on and off gradually. We use the "while" statement to do that.

To be able to see the dimming and brightening, you need to slow it down using the delay function or else you won't perceive the rapid flashing.

The Final Code

```
// variables
int led= 5; // the PMW pin the LED is connected to
int brightness = 255; // how bright the LED is
int fadeAmount =3; // the number of points to fade the LED by

void setup() // the setup function runs once when you press
reset or power the board
{
pinMode(led, OUTPUT); // initialize pin 5 as an output
}
void loop()  // the loop function runs repeatedly
```

```
{
 while(brightness != 0); //this loop is to decrease brightness
 {
  analogWrite(led, brightness);

 delay(2000); // wait for 2 seconds to see the dimming effect

 brightness = brightness - fadeAmount; // the brightness
decreases by 3 points
 }
 while((brightness <=255) && ( brightness >= 0)); //increase
brightness
 {
 analogWrite(led, brightness);
 delay(2000);  // wait for 2 seconds to see the LED bright up
again
 brightness= brightness + fadeAmount; // the brightness
increases by 3 points
 }
}
```

Your code should run with or without the descriptions included. However, if you are a bit confused by the descriptions, below is the clear code:

```
int led= 5;
int brightness = 255;
int fadeAmount =3;
void setup()
{
pinMode(led, OUTPUT);
}
void loop()
{
 while(brightness != 0);
 {
  analogWrite(led, brightness);
  delay(2000);
  brightness = brightness - fadeAmount;
 }
 while((brightness <=255) && ( brightness >= 0));
 {
  analogWrite(led, brightness);
  delay(2000);
  brightness= brightness + fadeAmount;
 }
}
```

Once you are done writing the code, upload it and watch the effects. You should see the LED start by dimming then brightening up again.

Project 4: Building a Trick or Smart Switch

In this project, we are going to demonstrate a switch. A switch is an electrical component that either completes or breaks a circuit. When you push it, the circuit works and when you release it, the circuit is broken. We will be using a small push-button to control an LED whereby each time you press the button, the LED is turned on if it was off, or off it was on.

Required Hardware

- Arduino Uno Board
- Breadboard
- Jumper Wires
- USB Cable
- One LED
- A push-button switch
- Two resistors: One of a 10k Ohm and another one of a 220 Ohm.

Procedure

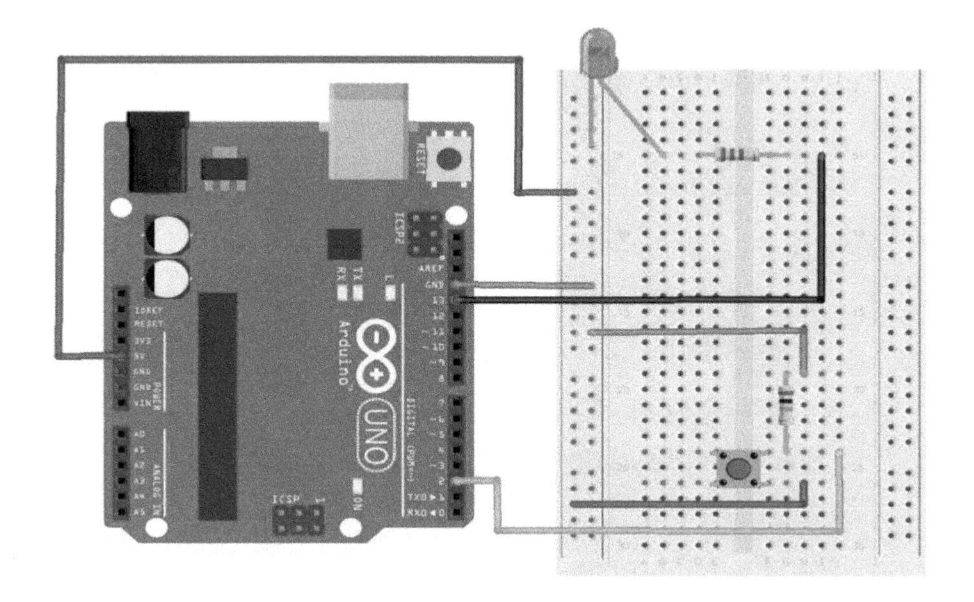

Step1: Wire Up Your Circuit and Components. Here are the steps:

- Connect your Arduino to the breadboard using a jumper wire. The wire should run from the GND on the Arduino to the GND rail on the breadboard.
- Connect another jumper wire between the GND rail on the breadboard and somewhere else on the same breadboard (you could put it at H19).
- Connect the red jumper wire so that it runs from the power rail to H26.
- Connect another jumper wire, the green one, so that it runs from pin 2 on the Arduino board to J24 on the breadboard.

- Put one leg of a 10k Ohm resistor at G19 on the breadboard and the other leg at G24.
- Connect your pushbutton switch. The switch should be placed into F24, into F26, into E24, and into E26.
- Connect the 220 Ohm resistor on the breadboard so that one leg goes in D5 and the other in G5.
- Connect your LED to the breadboard so that the shorter leg goes in the GND rail, and the longer leg goes in at B5.
- Connect another jumper wire (the black one) so that it runs from pin 13 on the Arduino board to cell I5 on the breadboard.
- Run the red jumper wire from 5V on the Arduino board to the power rail indicated by +.
- Lastly, use the USB cable to connect the Arduino board to your computer.

Step 2: Write your Sketch.

```
// Constants
const pushbuttonPin=2;      // the pin number the pushbutton
is connected to
const ledPin=13;                  // the pin number that the LED
is connected to
//Variables
Int pushbuttonState=0;                  // the current status of the
pushbutton
Void setup () {
```

```
PinMode (pushbuttonPin, INPUT);  // define the push button
as an input
PinMode (ledpin, OUTPUT);          // define the LED as an
output
digitalWrite(led,LOW);             //the LED should be turned
off for just in case
}
Void loop () {
pushbuttonState= digitalRead (pushbuttonPin);// read the
status of the pushbutton value
if (pushbuttonState == HIGH);   //  check if the pushbutton is
pressed
                                // if it is, the pushbutton
status is HIGH
 {
digitalWrite(ledPin, HIGH);     // turn on the LED
}
Else {                          // otherwise ....
 digitalWrite(ledPin, LOW);    // turn LED off
}
delay(2000);  // give the hardware two seconds to stabilize
then begin again
}
}
```

Below is a clear sketch of the same code if the comments within the code confuse you.

```
const pushbuttonPin=2;
const ledPin=13;
int pushbuttonState=0;
Void setup () {
PinMode (pushbuttonPin, INPUT);
PinMode (ledpin, OUTPUT);
digitalWrite(led,LOW);
}
Void loop () {
pushbuttonState= digitalRead (pushbuttonPin);
if (pushbuttonState == HIGH);
 {
digitalWrite(ledPin, HIGH);
}
Else {
 digitalWrite(ledPin, LOW);
}
delay(2000);
}
}
```

Step 3: Upload the Sketch. Upload the code above and observe. You should have a switch that turns on the LED when pressed and off when released.

Project 5: Sunrise-Sunset Light Switch

It is quite easy to design and build new electronic devices when you know the secret ingredients for rapid design. The trick behind it is to take the already existing electronic devices and make a slight change to them. For example, you can easily change the smart-switch device to a noncontact one by simply adding a sensor. In this case, you can build a sunrise-sunset light switch by making a few changes to the smart or trick switch project above.

The major change you are required to make is to use a photocell instead of the mini pushbutton. A photocell is a resistor that changes its resistance depending on the amount of light that touches its surface. Any light falling on a photocell decreases its value of resistance. The other change you will need to make is to add a green LED to pin D 13 on the Arduino. Therefore, to build this project, here are the things you will need:

Required Hardware

- 10K Ohm resistor
- 330 Ohm resistor
- Electrolytic capacitor (100uF)
- An Arduino board
- Full-size clear breadboard
- Photocell

- A green LED
- A red LED
- Connecting wires

Procedure

Step 1: Gather all the above parts and place them on your workbench or laboratory tabletop.

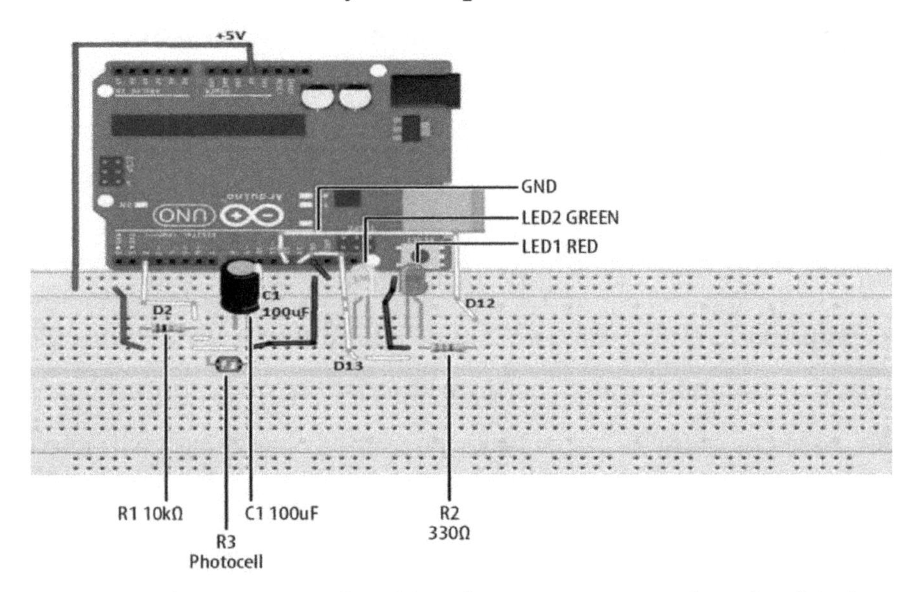

Step 2: Wire up your circuit and components using the fritzing diagram below:

Step 3: Write your sketch

// constants won't change:

const int photocellPin = 2; *// the pin number the photocell is connected to*

const int redledPin = 12; *// the pin number the red LED is connected to*

```
const int greenledPin = 13; // the pin number the onboard
LED and green LED is connected to
// variables will change:
int photocellStatus = 0; // the variable for reading the
photocell status

void setup() {
pinMode(redledPin, OUTPUT); // define the red LED as an
output
pinMode(greenledPin, OUTPUT); // define the green LED as
an output
pinMode(photocellPin, INPUT); // define the photocell sensor
as an input
}

void loop(){
photocellStatus= digitalRead(photocellPin); // read the status
of the photocell value
                                        // check if the
photocell/sensor is activated
if (photocellStatus == HIGH); // if the sensor is activated, the
photocell status is HIGH
{
digitalWrite(redledPin, HIGH); // turn red LED on
digitalWrite(greenledPin, LOW); // and turn off the green LED
}
```

```
else // otherwise...
{
digitalWrite(redledPin, LOW); // turn off the red LED
digitalWrite(greenledPin, HIGH); // and turn on the green LED
}
}
```

Step 4: Upload the sketch to the Arduino. The greed LED will turn on.

Step 5: Wave your hand over the photocell for a moment. The red LED should turn on after a few seconds, then it will turn back off, and the green LED will turn on.

Project 6: Wireless Doorbell

In most homes, a knock at the gate, or the door, works just as a doorbell. The concept advanced further by shifting to wired electronic doorbell devices that were being fixed in one place. As we all know, technology is developing fast and the traditional doorbell we had was replaced by modern, wireless doorbell devices. Wireless doorbells can be placed anywhere; their position is not fixed, and their installation is also pretty simple.

In this project, we are going to build a simple, wireless doorbell using the Arduino UNO board. The project demonstrates the RF module's implementation for wireless communication.

Required Hardware

- Arduino UNO board
- RF Transmitter Module (434 MHz)
- HT - 12D Decoder IC
- 33 KΩ Resistor
- Small Buzzer
- Breadboard
- HT - 12E Encoder IC
- Resistor (750 Ohm)
- Push Button
- Power Supply
- Connecting Wires

Procedure

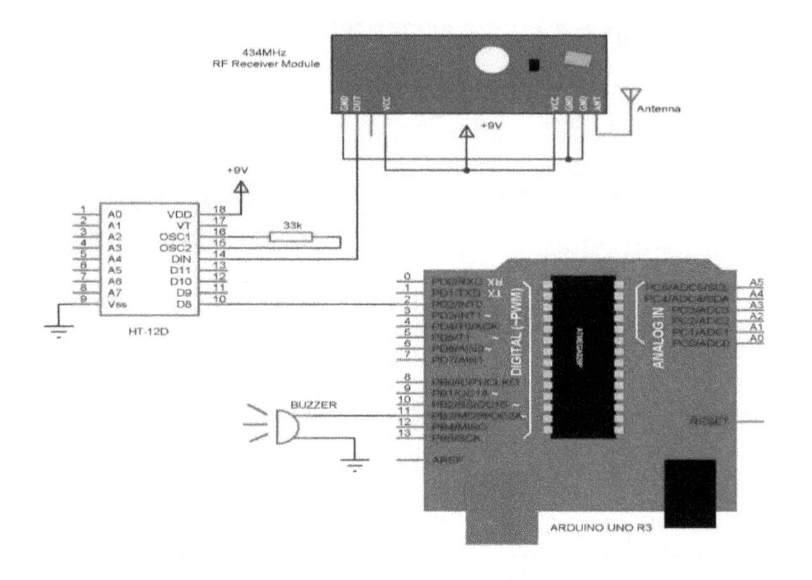

Step 1: Wire up the transmitter and receiver circuits. Here is the schematic diagram of how your circuits should look:

Step 2: Write the sketch of your code

```
// Constants
const pushbuttonPin=2;     // the pin number the pushbutton is
connected to
const buzzerPin=13;        // the pin number that the buzzer is
connected to

//Variables
int pushbuttonStatus=0;        // the current status of the
pushbutton
```

```
Void setup () {
PinMode (pushbuttonPin, INPUT);        // define the push
button as an input
PinMode (buzzerPin, OUTPUT);              // define the buzzer
as an output
}
Void loop () {
pushbuttonState= digitalRead (pushbuttonPin); // read the
status of the pushbutton

if (pushbuttonState == HIGH);           //  check if the
pushbutton is pressed
                                        // if it is, the pushbutton
status is HIGH
 {
digitalWrite(buzzerPin, HIGH);              // the buzzer will
produce sound
}
Else {  // otherwise ....
 digitalWrite(buzzerPin, LOW);           // the buzzer will not
produce sound
}
delay(3000);  // give the hardware three seconds to stabilize
then begin again
}
}
```

Step 3: Upload your sketch to the Arduino. If you connected the circuit properly and uploaded the correct sketch, the buzzer on the receiving end should start making a sound whenever you press the pushbutton at the transmitter end.

Advantages

- You can further extend this idea to a real-time, wireless doorbell system
- Its range is considerably large compared to other wireless technologies since it uses RF as the mode of communication.
- This project best suits homes, offices, garages, shops, and hospitals.

Chapter Nine: Troubleshooting and Fixing Arduino Issues

There are instances when you will experience problems or issues working with the Arduino program or hardware. The problem may be caused by hardware or software issues that will likely result in failure of proper functioning or the presence of errors. We are going to discuss how to troubleshoot and solve some of the most common Arduino software and hardware problems.

Having Issues Loading Programs on Arduino.

Once you have a well-written sketch together, loading it on the board shouldn't be a problem. However, there are several things that might get in the way of loading your codes into the system. Some of these reasons include:

- Missing the right drivers or having outdated ones
- Missing the right Arduino board configuration
- Using the wrong port
- Problematic physical connection of your circuit

Here are the solutions:

Solution 1: Check If Your Board Model Is the One Configured.

Double-checking the Arduino board that is configured should be the first thing you do when you experience loading problems. Sometimes you may select the wrong type of board on the program unknowingly. Just check to make sure that you have the right Arduino board configured and reload the code after verification to see if it works.

You also need to check the type of microcontroller on your board. Don't be confused, it is very simple. Check your board and spot the type of microcontroller it has and then select it from the device. The latest Arduino boards have an ATmega328 microcontroller.

Another common problem that may fail to load programs is missing drivers. Ensure that the board is connected to the computer and check whether the driver was installed. Go to the device manager in your computer and find out if there are some marked or unidentified items. The marked driver should be the one belonging to your Arduino board. The driver may not be updated, so you may need to update or reinstall it.

Solution 2: Make Sure Your Arduino Is Functioning.

An Arduino board must be powered for it to be detected by a computer. Ensure that the board is receiving electricity. Look at the board's LED, if it is not on then the system is not receiving any electricity. Once you notice this, the first thing to do is to check whether the power supply source is working. For those with Arduino boards that have dual power options, check if the jumper is able to get electricity from your desired source. If it doesn't, try disconnecting the device, then set the jumper to the power source and plug it again.

Solution 3: Reset the Device.

All Arduino boards have a reset button. This button is very helpful when you are experiencing problems while transferring your codes. Simply press the button and wait for a few seconds. Reload the program after the waiting time is up.

Solution 4: Diagnose the Physical Connection Problem.

Ensure that your board is on and connected to the computer. Check if the green LED is on to confirm this. In most cases, hardware connection is the prevalent cause of inconsistencies. A code cannot be uploaded if the pathway itself is busted. To solve this:

- Try a different USB cable; sometimes they just don't work.
- Check whether the serial port that should be assigned to your board is present or not.
- Ensure that the board is not touching anything conductive or metallic.
- Try disconnecting the digital pins 0 and 1 while uploading the program.
- Buy an original USB cable that is specifically meant for data transmission.
- Try changing the USB ports. Use a different USB port and see if it works. If it doesn't, try connecting it to another computer. If it works on another computer, then have your computer USB ports inspected.

Arduino Software is Not Working

If you have software incompatibility issues, sometimes programs don't work as expected. An Arduino software that doesn't load properly is probably installed using a program version that is incompatible with the operating system.

Solution 1: Uninstall the Program.

Download the newer version that is compatible with your operating system, then reinstall.

Solution 2: Use a Third-Party Arduino Program.

Most third-party Arduino programs promoted by Arduino developers work properly. Try downloading a new installer from the third-party developer's website. Make sure you uninstall the current program first before downloading and installing a new one. If this doesn't work, download and install the actual Arduino program, then load the program to see if it works.

Crashing and Freezing Arduino Software

When the Arduino software freezes, there usually are some devices installed that are causing the issue.

Solution:

Load the MSConfig utility and disable startup services and programs. Restart your computer, and then load the Arduino program. If the software loads flawlessly, then one of your startup programs may be causing the problem. To identify the service or program with the issue, test each of them individually.

Installed COM ports may confuse you and lead you to choose the wrong one, which will end up meddling with the loading process.

Other Solutions:

- Check and select the right COM port for your Arduino.
- Switch off your computer and unplug all other devices.
- Turn the computer on, then plug the device, and load the program to see if it is working.

Bootloader Problem

The Arduino bootloader allows the microcontroller board to read a program. This vital piece of code also enables you to make changes to your codes and re-upload them. Your Arduino can't perform these two functions if the bootloader has a problem.

Solution:

To solve this problem, you have to understand that the firmware (A.K.A. the bootloader software) is no longer working. Therefore, the clear solution is to replace the firmware. To do this, simply download the Arduino bootloader file from the Arduino developer's website and upload it to the board.

Grounding Errors

It is very important to ensure correct grounding, as it saves your project from unexpected power surges and damage. Any Arduino grounding issue needs to be fixed as soon as it is noticed; if not, your board may get fried.

Solution:

Use a voltmeter to check the GND pin voltage.

Helpful Tips for Beginners

- **Don't dispose or throw away damaged Arduino boards.** If you are a beginner, the chances of damaging your board are high. Don't fret because it is part of the learning process. Don't throw the board away if you do damage it. Instead, dismantle its parts and get familiarized with them. Learn how each piece was installed. This will help you avoid further damage in the future and also will teach you how to create your own custom board.
- **Take note of extra or missing code characters**. It is easy to add or leave out some characters while coding. This mistake prevents the system from generating the desired results. It is very important to double-check the code and remove any extra characters or add any missing ones before uploading it. Always remember to put a semicolon at the end of each line of code as it is mandatory.
- **Take advantage of the Serial.list() command.** For Arduino code to function, the program has to read the board from the right port. The easiest way to verify your

configuration is by typing the Serial.list() command. This lists all of the available ports on your board.

- **Add notes on the codes if necessary.** Adding notes on your codes helps you remember the results they should generate. Write a note beside a line of code by typing a space, then two slashes (//), followed by the note. The slashes indicate that the next characters are not part of the code. Therefore, the system will not try to interpret your notes and meddle with your project results. Here is an example: ***delay(2000); // wait for 2 seconds to see the dimming effect***

- **Take precautionary measures while assembling.** Arduino installation requires safe handling; it's easy to damage it or cause an accident. Assembling your circuit can burn and wound your hands and fingers. To avoid these unfortunate scenarios, follow soldering and building guides closely.

Conclusion

The beauty of Arduino is in trying out different projects. The most amazing thing about this type of program is that you can easily get a simple project up and running, even if you don't have any knowledge or experience with electronics or programming. But now that you have read the basics in this book, you have more than what it takes to build your own Arduino projects. The next step is to start making your own sketches.

When you get ideas for the new projects you might want to try from your local hobby store or from your friends, consider joining a community. You might find robots interesting and decide to join an online robotics community, for example. Building projects with friends and comparing them to each other makes it more fun and motivating. If you feel like you don't know where to start, don't worry, because there are so many online sources that share coding and techniques to improve your programming game. Arduino is so famous and widely used that there are many online sites that have dedicated forums that are specifically tailored to help people learn Arduino programming and electronics.

If you wish to start a project, but you are feeling strapped for cash, don't give up because there are still options for you. As I said earlier, Arduino has been in place for quite a long time; nowadays, it is widely manufactured and sometimes fabricated in multiple versions by third-party manufacturers. This means that there are fairly cheap modules for purchase. Inexpensive and even free programming languages are also available for download on Arduino sites. Learning these languages is pretty easy, and if you know even one programming language, then you are good to go! If you don't know any, there are several ways that you can learn. You can get free programming books at your local library, and if you get stuck, you can go online and ask for help from other developers who have worked with Arduino and know how to get you started.

Key Takeaways

- The Arduino programming language is exactly like C++; it has two major functions, or rather, sections: the setup () and loop ().
- The variables are initialized within the setup () function. The loop () function on the other hand is where the magic happens; it contains the blocks of code that run repeatedly.
- Arduino boards have different numbers of pins depending on the model. Each of these pins has a unique number that identifies them.
- When coding, you have to specify the pin number you are working with.

- Once you get your Arduino board, you have to set up the Arduino IDE on your computer.
- All your codes should be written on the IDE before they are uploaded on to the board.
- You must power up the Arduino board before use. Some board models need to be configured to allow power to be taken from the computer.
- Plans for Arduino code are commonly known as sketches.
- You must upload your sketch to the board by clicking the upload button for you to see its effects.
- The Arduino board has many sensors, so ensure you check which one you would like to employ.

Arduinos are used in classrooms all over the world as a starter to programming and electronics. They are very user-friendly and the greatest part of owning one is that you get a chance to explore ideas and experiment. You are not limited here. You can easily come up with your own ways to make machines work; just start with simple projects like blinking or fading an LED and see what you can do from there.

I have included some codes for simple projects for you to try out and the steps to set them up, but I also recommend that you go and find some of your own. There are many sources and guides that can help, and you can also check out some more advanced projects and concepts that we didn't have a chance to touch on here. The Arduino board is really incredible. There is a lot you can do with it. Just pick a direction that interests you and see how far you can take the board. I hope that having read this book, you will go out there, try new things, and see the capabilities of your sketch designing skills. Arduino boards are an entertaining way to get started on your programming journey!

References

(2016). *Arduino - Quick Guide*. Tutorials Point. Arduino - Quick Guide (tutorialspoint.com)

Boxall, J. (2021). *Arduino Workshop, 2nd Edition: A Hands-on Introduction with 65 Projects* (2nd ed.). No Starch Press.

Dukish, B. (2018). *Coding the Arduino: Building Fun Programs, Games, and Electronic Projects (Technology in Action)* (1st ed.). Apress.

G. (2021, February 11). *Arduino Traffic Light Project*. Pi My Life Up. https://pimylifeup.com/arduino-traffic-light-project/

Géron, D. (2021). *Arduino Programming: The Ultimate Guide for Absolute Beginners with Steps to Learn Arduino Programming and The Fundamental Electronic Concepts*. Tiger Gain Ltd.

Getting Started with the Arduino GSM Shield. (2021). Arduino Documentation. https://docs.arduino.cc/retired/getting-started-guides/ArduinoGSMShield/

Gold, S. (2017). *Arduino: Taking The Next Step With Arduino: The Ultimate Beginner's Guide - Part 2 (Arduino 101,*

Arduino sketches, Complete beginners guide, . . . c++, Ruby, html, php, Programming Robots). CreateSpace Independent Publishing Platform.

Instructables. (2017, October 8). *Arduino - Blinking LED.* https://www.instructables.com/Arduino-Blinking-LED/

Instructables. (2020, July 21). *How to Make Sunrise and Sunset Light Switch Sensor.* https://www.instructables.com/How-to-Make-Sunrise-and-Sunset-Light-Switch-Sensor/

Kaswan, K. et. al. (2020, January). *Role of Arduino in Real World Applications.* (Vol. 9, Issue 01). International Journal of Scientific & Technology Research.

Makerspaces.com. (2018, February 13). *Simple Arduino Projects For Beginners.* https://www.makerspaces.com/simple-arduino-projects-beginners/

Monk, S. (2011). *Arduino + Android Projects for the Evil Genius: Control Arduino with Your Smartphone or Tablet* (1st ed.). McGraw-Hill Education TAB.

Monk, S. (2016a). *Programming Arduino: Getting Started with Sketches, Second Edition (Tab)* (2nd ed.). McGraw-Hill Education TAB.

Monk, S. (2016b). *Programming Arduino: Getting Started with Sketches, Second Edition (Tab)* (2nd ed.). McGraw-Hill Education TAB.

Monk, S. (2018). *Programming Arduino Next Steps: Going Further with Sketches, Second Edition* (2nd ed.). McGraw-Hill Education TAB.

Nicholas, S. (2020). *Arduino Programming: A Comprehensive Beginner's Guide to learn the Realms of Arduino from A-Z.* Independently published.

Parker, D. (2020). *Arduino Programming: The Ultimate Guide For Making the Best of Your Arduino Programming Projects.* New Begin Ltd.

Ryan, T. (2019). *Arduino Programming: The Ultimate Beginner's Guide to Learn Arduino Programming Step by Step.* nelly B.L. International Consulting LTD.

Wilcher, D. (n.d.). *Make: Basic Arduino Projects: 26 Experiments with Microcontrollers and Electronics (Chinese Edition).* MARKER MEDIA.

Wilcher, D. (2014). *Basic Arduino Projects: 26 Experiments with Microcontrollers and Electronics (Make: Technology on Your Time)* (1st ed.). Make Community, LLC.

Image Credit: Shutterstock.com